G000166946

THIS BOOK BELONGS TO...

Name: | Age:

Favourite player:

2020/2021

My Predictions...   **Actual...**

The Foxes' final position:

The Foxes' top scorer:

Premier League winners:

Premier League top scorer:

FA Cup winners:

EFL Cup winners:

Contributors: Peter Rogers

A TWOCAN PUBLICATION

©2020. Published by twocan under licence from Leicester City FC.

ISBN 978-1-913362-31-7

PICTURE CREDITS: Leicester City FC, Action Images and Press Association.

CONTENTS

TEAM 2020/21

KASPER 01
SCHMEICHEL

POSITION: Goalkeeper **DOB:** 05/11/1986
COUNTRY: Denmark

A Premier League champion with the Foxes in 2015/16, goalkeeper Kasper Schmeichel is now closing in on 400 career appearances for Leicester City.

Firmly established as the club's first choice stopper, following his arrival from Leeds United in the summer of 2011. Schmeichel is in fact a two-time title winner with the Foxes, having also been Championship title winner in 2013/14.

JAMES 02
JUSTIN

POSITION: Defender **DOB:** 23/02/1998
COUNTRY: England

Blessed with the flexibility to operate in either full-back berth, defender James Justin joined the Foxes from Luton Town in the summer of 2019 having helped the Hatters secure promotion to the Championship.

Ironically his Leicester City debut came against his former club and he marked the occasion with a goal in a 4-0 League Cup triumph. The full-back also enjoyed a winning start to his Premier League career as Leicester defeated Watford 2-0 in December 2019.

04 ÇAĞLAR
SÖYÜNCÜ

POSITION: Defender **DOB:** 23/05/1996
COUNTRY: Turkey

Following the transfer of Harry Maguire to Manchester United, Turkish international Çağlar Söyüncü formed an excellent central defensive partnership with Jonny Evans as the Foxes made a flying start to the 2019/20 Premier League season.

Blessed with great strength in the tackle and with superb composure on the ball, Söyüncü's performances won him many admirers last season as he swiftly gained a reputation as one of the Premier League's best defenders.

WESLEY 03
FOFANA

POSITION: Defender **DOB:** 17/12/2000
COUNTRY: France

Widely regarded as one of the hottest young prospects in French football, defender Wesley Fofana joined Leicester City from Saint Etienne on 2 October 2020.

The teenager agreed a five-year deal the King Power Stadium after his fierce and committed performances in Ligue 1 won him many admirers. Having been capped by France at under-21 level, Fofana will be hopeful a successful Premier League move could help escalate him into the senior France squad.

KELECHI
IHEANACHO

SOCCER SKILLS

Great goalkeepers are an essential ingredient for successful teams in today's game. They have to excel in all areas of the art of 'keeping and Kasper Schmeichel is a great 'keeper that lives up to these expectations.

DISTRIBUTION
THE BASICS OF GOOD THROWING TECHNIQUE

OVERARM THROW

This is best for covering long distances. The body should be in line with the direction of the throw with the weight on the back foot. The ball should be brought forward in a bowling action with the arm straight.

JAVELIN THROW

This throw is made quickly with a low trajectory. The arm is bent for this throw, the ball is held beside the head and the body is in line with the direction of the throw. The arm is brought forward in a pushing movement with the ball being released at the top.

UNDERARM THROW

The ball is released from a crouching position, with a smooth underarm swing.

Throws do not usually travel as far as kicks but the greater speed and accuracy of throwing can make up for the lack of distance and will help the team retain possession. A player receiving a throw must be able to control it early.

Work hard at distribution and the benefits of this will be seen whenever you are in possession during a match.

EXERCISE ONE
Grab a friend and throw the ball to each other using the various throwing techniques at various distances apart.

EXERCISE TWO
The goalkeeper with the ball uses the various throws to knock another ball off a marker.

EXERCISE THREE
The goalkeepers try to throw the ball through the markers using various throwing techniques.

BOYS OF

2000

Under the charismatic management of Martin O'Neill, Leicester City enjoyed a highly successful 1999/2000 season with the Foxes securing an eighth-place finish in the Premier League and winning the League Cup for the second time in four seasons.

The pursuit of League Cup glory began with a two-legged second round meeting with Crystal Palace. It really was a case of goals galore against the Nationwide First Division Eagles as a 3-3 draw at Selhurst Park was followed by a 4-2 win at Filbert Street which saw O'Neill's men run out 7-5 winners on aggregate.

Goals from Muzzy Izzet and Emile Heskey saw the Foxes overcome Grimsby Town at home in the third round to a tee-up an all-Premier League tie away to Leeds United in round four.

STAR PERFORMER
MATT ELLIOTT

Big players often come to the fore in big games and that was certainly the case for defender Matt Elliott in the Foxes' 1999/2000 League Cup campaign.

A regular on Martin O'Neill's teamsheet in the Premier League, Elliott made six League Cup appearances in 1999/2000 and weighed in with three vital goals. The powerful central defender scored the winning goal in the semi-final second leg against Aston Villa to propel the Foxes to Wembley and then produced a two-goal Man of the Match performance in the final.

He opened the scoring in the 29th minute at Wembley and after former Foxes' striker David Kelly levelled for Tranmere, Elliott became the hero of the hour by netting the winner nine minutes from time to seal a 2-1 Wembley victory.

There was literally nothing between the two sides at Elland Road and with neither side able to forge a breakthrough the match was decided by penalties. The Foxes held their nerve and won the shootout 4-2.

Leicester had home advantage and lower league opposition at the quarter-final stage when they were paired with Fulham. The Cottagers rose to the occasion and a thrilling 90 minutes ended 2-2 before 30 minutes extra-time produced a goal apiece. With the score level at 3-3 after 120 minutes of pulsating cup action, it once again came down to spot-kicks. Again the Foxes progressed from the shootout, this time 3-0.

O'Neill's men then saw off Midlands rivals Aston Villa 1-0 in a two-legged semi-final to land a Wembley date with Tranmere Rovers.

In front of almost 75,000 at Wembley, the Foxes defeated a battling Tranmere Rovers side to secure the League Cup and a place in the UEFA Cup the following season.

WES 05 MORGAN

POSITION: Defender   **DOB:** 21/01/1984
COUNTRY: Jamaica

Club captain Wes Morgan agreed a new one-year contract with the Foxes to extend his stay at the King Power Stadium until the summer of 2021, which will result in ten years service at the club.

Having led the team to Premier League success in 2015/16, Morgan's experience and know-how sees him remain an important member of the Leicester squad. He made 17 appearances in all competitions in 2019/20.

JONNY 06 EVANS

POSITION: Defender   **DOB:** 03/01/1988
COUNTRY: Northern Ireland

Ultra-reliable central defender Jonny Evans produced a number of polished performances at the heart of the Foxes' defence alongside Çağlar Söyüncü in 2019/20 as Europa League football was secured for the 2020/21 campaign.

The experienced Northern Ireland international, who joined from West Bromwich Albion in the summer of 2018 for a bargain £3.5M, made his 400th appearance in English football in July 2020.

07 DEMARAI
GRAY

POSITION: Midfielder   **DOB:** 28/06/1996
COUNTRY: England

England under-21 international Demarai Gray made 29 appearances for Brendan Rodgers' side in 2019/20 as the Foxes secured fifth place in the Premier League and reached the latter stages of both domestic cup competitions.

The winger's ability to run at opponents with the ball continues to impress the Leicester City faithful and makes him one of the club's most exciting talents. He netted three goals in 2019/20 including the winner away to West Ham United.

GOAL
OF THE SEASON

HARVEY BARNES

V SHEFFIELD UNITED

24 AUGUST 2019

There were several special strikes among the Foxes' 67 Premier League goals in 2019/20 but when it came to voting for the club's official Goal of the Season - Harvey Barnes' magnificent first-time volley against Sheffield United in August 2019 topped the poll.

Voted by the club's supporters, the prestigious Goal of the Season award was one of two accolades that Barnes was presented with at the end of the campaign, with the exciting winger also landing the club's Young Player of the Year award too.

His stunning strike at Bramall Lane back in the August sunshine was the first of seven goals he went on to net in the 2019/20 campaign and it secured the Foxes their first Premier League win of the season.

Having shared the spoils with Wolverhampton Wanderers (0-0) and Chelsea (1-1), Brendan Rodgers men looked all set for a third consecutive draw at the start of the season as they found themselves on level terms at 1-1 with the newly-promoted Blades. Jamie Vardy had seen his first-half strike cancelled out by Oli McBurnie shortly after the hour. However, parity did not last for long as substitute Barnes, who had only been on the pitch six minutes, struck an unforgettable winner with 20 minutes remaining.

Barnes found himself in the right place at the right time to fire home a stunning volley from the edge of the box which flew past home 'keeper Dean Henderson and thrilled the travelling Foxes fans massed behind the goal.

If ever there was a goal worthy of winning a game then this was certainly it.

The goal clearly gave Barnes the taste for more and after scoring in the FA Cup victory over Wigan Athletic he then added Premier League goals against Burnley, West Ham United, Chelsea and Aston Villa (two) in a highly impressive campaign for the Academy graduate.

Reflecting on his two awards, Barnes said:

"I've really enjoyed this season and, with the support of the manager and, of course, the fans, I feel that I've been able to improve my game."

Challenge your favourite grown-up and find out which of you is the biggest Premier League brain!

ADULTS

Who is the captain of Wolverhampton Wanderers?

1 ANSWER

Can you name the four Premier League clubs that reached the 2019/20 FA Cup semi-finals?

2 ANSWER

At which club did Chelsea boss Frank Lampard begin his managerial career?

3 ANSWER

Who is the oldest manager in the Premier League?

4 ANSWER

At which club did Southampton's star striker Danny Ings begin his career?

5 ANSWER

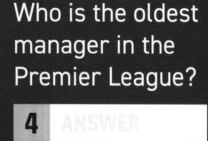

From which club did Manchester United sign Bruno Fernandes?

6 ANSWER

At which club did Newcastle manager Steve Bruce begin his playing career?

7 ANSWER

How many clubs from the north west have won the Premier League title?

8 ANSWER

Who were the first London club to win the Premier League?

9 ANSWER

Which Premier League manager is also his club's record goalscorer?

10 ANSWER

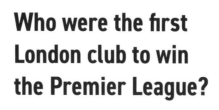

V KIDS

The adults' questions are on the left page and the kids' questions are on the right page.

Which team began the 2020/21 Premier League season as defending champions for the first time?

1 ANSWER

What nationality is Chelsea striker Timo Werner?

2 ANSWER

How many Premier League clubs have the title 'United' in their name?

3 ANSWER

Who plays their home games at Molineux?

4 ANSWER

Which Premier League ground has the largest capacity?

5 ANSWER

Which current Premier League club won last season's League Cup?

6 ANSWER

What is Everton's nickname?

7 ANSWER

Can you name the club that play their home matches at St James' Park?

8 ANSWER

Who is the manager of Burnley?

9 ANSWER

What nationality is Tottenham Hotspur manager Jose Mourinho?

10 ANSWER

Fill the page with your footy goals and dreams, no matter how big or small, and then start working on how to accomplish them!

We've started you off...

1. Visit the King Power Stadium

2. Complete 50 keepy-uppies

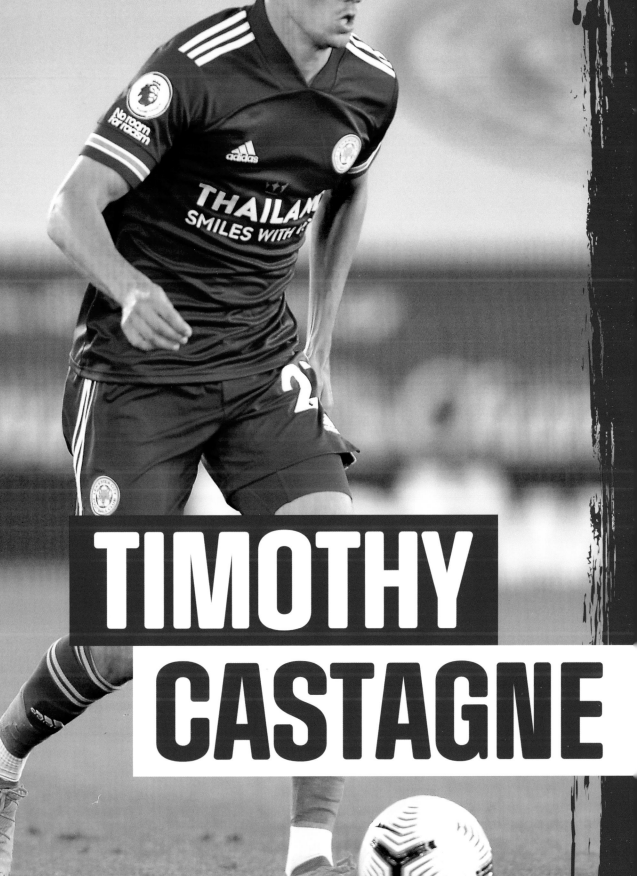

TIMOTHY
CASTAGNE

1

3

4

5

WHO ARE YER?

Can you figure out the identity of all these Foxes stars?

6

7

8

9

10

TEAM 2020/21

YOURI 08
TIELEMANS

POSITION: Midfielder   **DOB:** 07/05/1997
COUNTRY: Belgium

Alongside James Maddison, midfielder Youri Tielemans helps provide the creative spark in the Foxes' team and his ability to engineer chances for others plus contribute with goals of his own make him a real match winner.

A full Belgian international, Tielemans was signed from Monaco following a successful loan spell at the King Power and scored six goals for club and country in the 2019/20 season.

JAMIE 09
VARDY

POSITION: Striker   **DOB:** 11/01/1987
COUNTRY: England

Crowd favourite Jamie Vardy enjoyed another sensational scoring season for the Foxes in 2019/20 and ended the campaign as the club's Player of the Season.

The livewire striker netted 23 Premier League goals to propel Leicester City into the 2020/21 Europa League. He also topped the Premier League scoring charts landing him the prestigious Golden Boot award at the end of the season.

10 JAMES MADDISON

POSITION: Midfielder   **DOB:** 23/11/1996
COUNTRY: England

Midfield playmaker James Maddison has been a star performer at the King Power Stadium since his move from Norwich City in the summer of 2018.

The 2019/20 season saw his excellent club form for the Foxes rewarded with a first full England cap after the creative midfielder made his Three Lions' bow as a substitute in England's 7-0 victory over Montenegro in a European Championship qualifier at Wembley in November 2019. To the delight of all Foxes' fans, Maddison agreed an extended contract with the club in August 2020.

MARC 11 ALBRIGHTON

POSITION: Midfielder   **DOB:** 18/11/1989
COUNTRY: England

Marc Albrighton's Leicester City career has coincided with the most successful period in the club's history.

Having joined the Foxes in 2014 from Midlands rivals Aston Villa, the midfielder played a key role in the team's top-flight survival in 2014/15 before going on to feature in every Premier League game in 2015/16 as Leicester landed the title. Last season saw him make 28 appearances for Brendan Rodgers' side and take his Foxes' career tally to over 200 games.

PREPARING
FOR ACTION

Football matches may well be scheduled for 90 minutes but there are many days of preparation that go into making sure that Brendan Rodgers' men are at their physical and mental peak when they cross the white line to represent Leicester City Football Club.

Like all Premier League clubs, the Foxes' pre-match planning is meticulous. The manager of course has final say as to who makes his starting line-up but the boss is ably assisted by a backroom staff of coaches, sports scientists, strength and conditioning experts, physiotherapists and nutritionists who all play their part in helping fine tune the players ahead of the manager's team selection.

The majority of the squads' preparations take place at the club's training ground and that all begins when the players report back for pre-season training.

Although the modern-day player has little down-time in terms of maintaining his overall fitness, pre-season really is a vital time for footballers to build themselves up to remain as fit, strong and healthy as possible for the challenging season that awaits.

The pre-season schedule often begins with a series of fitness tests. The results of those tests enables the club's coaching and fitness staff to assess each player's condition and level of fitness to ensure they are given the right work load during the pre-season programme.

When it comes to winning football matches, it is well known that both hard work and practice are two essential ingredients to success. However, in terms of strength and fitness, then rest, recovery and diet also have crucial parts to play in a footballer's wellbeing.

The modern game now sees technology playing its part in training too - prior to beginning their training sessions, the players are provided with a GPS tracking system and heart rate analysis monitors ensuring that all that they do in a training session can be measured, monitored and reviewed.

On-pitch training drills and gym work is now enhanced further with players often taking part in yoga and pilates classes while always receiving expert advice in terms of their diet, rest and mental welfare.

YOURI TIELEMANS

SOCCER SKILLS
DEFENDING

Defending is an art - not as spectacular as swerving a free kick around the wall into the net or floating a crossfield pass into the path of an oncoming wingback - but nevertheless, just as important. Every successful team has a solid defence and can defend as a team.

Defenders must also master the art of defending one on one...

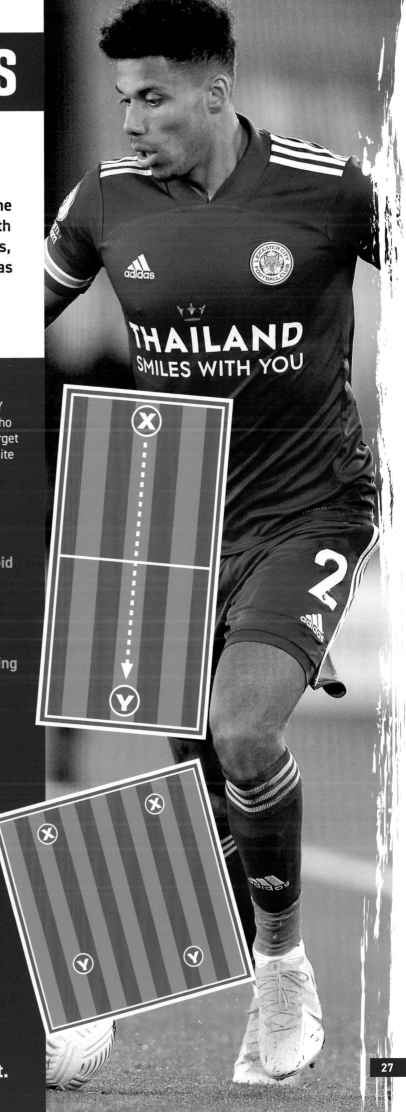

EXERCISE ONE

Two adjacent 10m x 10m grids have two players, X and Y at the opposite ends of the grids. X plays the ball to Y, who is then allowed to attack defender X with the ball. Y's target is to be able to stop the ball, under control, on the opposite end line. Defender X has to try to stop this happening. Y is encouraged to be direct and run at X with the ball.

KEY FACTORS

1. Do not approach the attacker square on. Adopt a sideways stance which enables rapid forward and backwards movement.

2. Do not dive in. Be patient and wait for your opponent to make a mistake. Always be on your toes.

3. Threaten the ball without actually committing to a tackle. Pretending to tackle can often panic the opponent!

4. Tackle when you are sure you will win it!

EXERCISE TWO

Here the game is progressed to a two v two situation when X1 and X2 play as a team against Y1 and Y2.

The same target is used for this game - the players have to stand on the opposite line with the ball, either by dribbling past their opponents or by passing the ball through them.

The same key factors are relevant here with the addition of two more:

5. Covering your defending partner when he is being attacked.

6. Communication between the two defenders is vital.

If a team can get these points of defending right, throughout the side, they will become very difficult to beat.

Take our quick-fire personality test to see where Brendan Rodgers would utilise your skills in the Foxes line-up...

WHICH FOOTBALLER ARE YOU?

1. What is your favourite activity at the park?

a. Leaping around
b. Practicing my heading
c. Lots of non-stop running
d. Scoring goals

2. What is your biggest strength?

a. My height
b. My strength
c. My stamina
d. My speed

3. Which would you rather win?

a. A game of catch
b. A weight lifting contest
c. A long distance run
d. A sprint race

4. You score a goal! How do you celebrate?

a. I turn and punch the air
b. I clench my fist in delight
c. I high-five a teammate
d. I slide on my knees

5. How would the opposition describe you?

a. Hard to beat
b. Determined to succeed
c. All-action
d. Lethal in front of goal

6. What's your favourite move?

a. Springing high to catch under pressure
b. A sliding tackle
c. Playing the perfect through ball
d. Spinning away from my marker

7. What is the key to winning a game?

a. Keeping a clean sheet

b. Winning your individual battles

c. Maintaining possession

d. Taking chances that come your way

MOSTLY As

You would clearly be a safe pair of hands in goal. Watch out Kasper Schmeichel, there's competition for the No1 shirt!

8. What is your favourite number?

a. One

b. Five

c. Seven

d. Nine

MOSTLY Bs

Sounds like you are a young James Justin in the making - there could well be a role for you in the Foxes back four...

MOSTLY Cs

You could comfortably take your place in the heart of midfield and help make things tick. Move over Youri Tielemans!

9. How would you describe your style of play?

a. Disciplined

b. Fully committed

c. Relentless

d. Technically gifted

10. What do your teammates call you?

a. Secure

b. Reliable

c. Energetic

d. Mr/Miss goals

MOSTLY Ds

Looks like we have a budding Jamie Vardy on our hands! Who do you fancy partnering in attack?

TEAM 2020/21

DANNY 12 WARD

POSITION: Goalkeeper **DOB:** 22/06/1993
COUNTRY: Wales

Danny Ward is one of three international goalkeepers vying for the number one spot at the King Power Stadium.

The Welsh stopper joined Leicester City in the summer of 2018 from Liverpool and has excelled when called upon in cup competitions. He marked his Foxes' debut with a League Cup clean sheet against Fleetwood Town before becoming the penalty shoot-out hero with three saves as Wolves were dispatched in 2018/19. Last season saw Ward register three impressive shut-outs from his four cup outings.

14 KELECHI IHEANACHO

POSITION: Striker **DOB:** 03/10/1996
COUNTRY: Nigeria

A full Nigerian international, striker Kelechi Iheanacho adds real depth and quality to the Foxes' forward options.

The former Manchester City man, who joined Leicester City in the summer of 2017, netted ten goals in all competitions for Brendan Rodgers' side in 2019/20, including a dramatic last-gasp winner against Everton at the King Power in December 2019.

HARVEY 15
BARNES

POSITION: Midfielder **DOB:** 09/12/1997
COUNTRY: England

Following loan spells at MK Dons, Barnsley and West Bromwich Albion, Academy graduate Harvey Barnes enjoyed a highly impressive 2019/20 season for the Foxes.

The attacking midfielder made 42 appearances in all competitions for Brendan Rodgers' team and was voted the club's Young Player of the Season. His stunning goal in the 2-1 win away to Sheffield United also saw him land the Foxes' Goal of the Season award.

16 FILIP
BENKOVIC

POSITION: Defender **DOB:** 13/07/1997
COUNTRY: Croatia

A full Croatian international, defender Filip Benkovic joined Leicester City in the summer of 2018 from Dinamo Zagreb.

The 23-year-old central defender boasts Champions League experience from his time with Zagreb and has developed his football education further with beneficial loan spells at Celtic and Bristol City since arriving at the King Power. His Foxes' debut came in the 2018/19 League Cup victory over Fleetwood Town.

BOYS OF 2009

Despite finding themselves in the third tier of English football for the first time in their history, Leicester City made a swift return to the Championship by winning the League One title at a canter in 2008/09.

Nigel Pearson was appointed manager and enjoyed a winning start to life in the Foxes' dugout as a Matty Fryatt brace secured an opening day 2-0 victory at home to MK Dons.

The Foxes impressed with a 4-0 win away to Cheltenham Town on 30 August and ended the month with three wins and a draw from their opening four League One fixtures.

Winning matches certainly became a nice habit for the Foxes and when Lloyd Dyer struck a last-minute winner in a five-goal thriller away to Huddersfield Town in October they were certainly looking the real deal.

STAR PERFORMER

MATTY FRYATT

Striker Matty Fryatt was clearly the standout performer in the Foxes' 2008/09 League One title-winning season.

The ace poacher certainly set his stall out for the season when he notched both goals in the opening day win over MK Dons. Those two goals proved to be the first of a 32-goal season, 27 of which came in the league.

Fryatt's goal-laden campaign saw him become the first Leicester player to score over 30 goals in a season since legendary striker, Arthur Rowley 52 years earlier. His impressive form also saw him voted the best player in League One at the 2008/09 Football League Awards.

The side engineered a 23-game unbeaten run between 1 November and 7 March, by which time they were well on course for promotion.

Following a hard-fought 1-0 win at home to fellow promotion hopefuls Leeds United, promotion and the title were confirmed in the following match at Southend United. Fryatt was the two-goal hero as his second-half brace saw off the Shrimpers and enabled the travelling Foxes' fans to celebrate by the seaside.

Leicester ended the season with a club record 96-point haul and a plus-45 goal difference as they landed the title ahead of runners-up Peterborough United.

COLOUR

JAMIE

VARDY

34

JAMES
JUSTIN

PLAYER OF THE SEASON

JAMIE VARDY

It was a case of honours galore for Foxes' striker Jamie Vardy come the end of the 2019/20 season at the King Power Stadium.

The ace marksman netted 23 Premier League goals as the Foxes secured fifth place in the table and ensured European football would return to Leicester for 2020/21. Ahead of the final game of the season, the club's supporters voted Vardy their Player of the Season.

Fans and players were clearly in agreement about Vardy's impressive contribution to the club's success in 2019/20 as the squad voted him the Players' Player of the Season too.

Vardy's 23-goal haul proved enough for him to top the Premier League scoring charts after edging out the 22-goal efforts of Southampton's Danny Ings and Arsenal's Pierre-Emerick Aubameyang. The Foxes' crowd favourite then adding the coveted Golden Boot Award to his growing collection of end-of-season gongs.

The striker first hit the goal trail for 2019/20 in the Foxes' 2-1 win away to Sheffield United in August 2019 before adding double strikes against Bournemouth, Aston Villa (twice), Newcastle United, and Crystal Palace. He also hammered home a hat-trick in the memorable 9-0 victory away to Southampton in October.

During the Foxes' home match with Crystal Palace in July 2020, Vardy netted his 100th Premier League goal and became only the 29th player to score a century of Premier League goals since the competition began in 1992. His landmark goal made the score 2-0 and he then notched Premier League goal number 101 in the final minute of the game to secure a 3-0 victory over the Eagles.

YOUNG PLAYER OF THE SEASON

HARVEY BARNES

Academy graduate Harvey Barnes landed the club's Young Player of the Season award after supporters voted him their top performing young Fox for 2019/20. The award capped off an excellent season for the Burnley-born winger who scored six goals and assisted in eight for Brendan Rodgers' side.

With the exciting ability to run at opponents and shoot from distance, Barnes' skills have made his a firm favourite at the King Power Stadium. After gaining valuable experience with loan spells at MK Dons, Barnsley and West Bromwich Albion, the Leicester youngster is now making his mark with his parent club and at the highest level.

AYOZE 17 PEREZ

POSITION: Striker **DOB:** 29/07/1993
COUNTRY: Spain

Spanish striker Ayoze Perez enjoyed an impressive first season with the Foxes following his arrival from Premier League rivals Newcastle United in the summer of 2019.

Perez netted a hat-trick in the memorable 9-0 victory away to Southampton in October 2019 and then opened the scoring against his former employers on New Year's Day 2020 as the Foxes ran out comfortable 3-0 winners at St James' Park.

DANIEL 18 AMARTEY

POSITION: Defender **DOB:** 21/12/1994
COUNTRY: Ghana

Ghanaian international Daniel Amartey joined the Foxes during their 2015/16 Premier League title-winning campaign and debuted in a 1-0 victory over Norwich City at the King Power.

Signed from Copenhagen, Amartey can play in either defence or midfield. A broken ankle suffered against West Ham in October 2018 interrupted his progress at the club and he will now be looking for a return to full fitness and first team action in 2020/21.

CENGIZ 19 UNDER

POSITION: Midfielder **DOB:** 14/07/1997
COUNTRY: Turkey

A right winger who has a proven eye for goal, plus great ability to create chances for teammates, Cengiz Under joined the Foxes on a season-long loan from AS Roma in September 2020.

A Turkey international, Under has represented his country on over 20 occasions and made his Premier League debut for Leicester City against West Ham United on 20 September 2020.

HAMZA 20 CHOUDHURY

POSITION: Midfielder **DOB:** 01/10/1997
COUNTRY: England

Loughborough-born Hamza Choudhury was handed a place in the Foxes' starting line-up for the opening game of the 2019/20 Premier League campaign as Leicester welcomed Wolves to the King Power.

He went on to feature in a total of 29 games, 20 of which were in the Premier League. A season highlight would have been his first league goal for the Foxes which saw the team wrap up an emphatic 3-0 win away to Newcastle.

RICARDO 21 PEREIRA

POSITION: Defender **DOB:** 06/10/1993
COUNTRY: Portugal

A consistent performer for the Foxes, Ricardo Pereira has produced many impressive displays at right-back for the club following his transfer from Porto in the summer of 2018.

He ended his first season at the King Power by landing both the Player of the Season award and also the Players' Player of the Season accolade. He was an integral part of Brendan Rodgers' team last season when he made 33 first team appearances and scored four goals before an anterior cruciate ligament injury ended his season.

There are five Filbert Foxes hiding in the crowd as Leicester City fans celebrate winning the League Cup at Wembley in 2000. Can you find him?

CLASSIC FANTASTIC

JAMIE
VARDY

Can you find the eight differences between these two photos?

SPOT THE DIFFERENCE

43

Here are our predictions for the 2020/21 season, see if you agree!

2020/21

PREMIER LEAGUE

OUR PREDICTION FOR PREMIER LEAGUE WINNERS:
MANCHESTER CITY

YOUR PREDICTION:

OUR PREDICTION FOR PREMIER LEAGUE RUNNERS-UP:
LIVERPOOL

YOUR PREDICTION:

CHAMPIONSHIP

OUR PREDICTION FOR CHAMPIONSHIP WINNERS:
WATFORD

YOUR PREDICTION:

OUR PREDICTION FOR CHAMPIONSHIP RUNNERS-UP:
SWANSEA CITY

YOUR PREDICTION:

TOP SCORERS

OUR PREDICTION FOR PREMIER LEAGUE TOP SCORER:

JAMIE VARDY

YOUR PREDICTION:

OUR PREDICTION FOR CHAMPIONSHIP TOP SCORER:

IVAN TONEY

YOUR PREDICTION:

FA CUP & EFL CUP

OUR PREDICTION FOR FA CUP WINNERS:

LEICESTER CITY

YOUR PREDICTION:

OUR PREDICTION FOR EFL CUP WINNERS:

MIDDLESBROUGH

YOUR PREDICTION:

PREDICTIONS

MATTY 22
JAMES

POSITION: Midfielder   **DOB:** 22/07/1991
COUNTRY: England

Now one of the Foxes' longest-serving players, midfielder Matty James arrived at the King Power in May 2012 from Manchester United.

Together with Jamie Vardy, he enjoyed a goalscoring debut in a League Cup triumph away to Torquay United in August 2012 and has amassed over 100 appearances for the club. With first team football tough to come by, he was loaned to Barnsley in 2017.

24 NAMPALYS
MENDY

POSITION: Midfielder   **DOB:** 23/06/1992
COUNTRY: France

Defensive midfielder Nampalys Mendy joined the Foxes from Nice in the summer of 2016 following the club's 2015/16 Premier League title triumph.

His arrival at the King Power saw him briefly take the mantle of becoming the club's record signing. That tag lasted just five days before Ahmed Musa joined in a £16M deal. Mendy debuted at Wembley in the 2016/17 Charity Shield and in August 2020 he agreed a new two-year contract extension with the Foxes.

WILFRED `25`
NDIDI

POSITION: Midfielder   **DOB:** 16/12/1996
COUNTRY: Nigeria

A powerful performer in the heart of the Foxes' midfield, Nigerian international Wilfred Ndidi brings great tackling ability to the team and his combative nature has made him a real favourite at the King Power.

Ndidi joined Leicester City from Belgian side Genk in January 2017 and made such an impact that he landed the club's 2016/17 Young Player of the Season award in just half a season's action. He made 39 appearances in all competitions last season and netted the club's first Premier League goal of the 2019/20 campaign.

`26` DENNIS
PRAET

POSITION: Midfielder   **DOB:** 14/05/1994
COUNTRY: Belgium

Attacking midfielder Dennis Praet arrived at the King Power Stadium in the summer of 2019 following a successful three-year spell with Sampdoria.

A full Belgian international, Praet has a reputation for his ability to run at opponents with real intent and to then use his range of passing skills to create chances for teammates. He made 27 Premier League appearances for the Foxes in 2019/20 with his first goal for the club coming against Southampton in January 2020.

HARVEY
BARNES

SOCCER SKILLS
CHEST CONTROL

Controlling the ball quickly and with minimum fuss in order to get the ball where you want it, so you can pass or shoot, can be the difference between a good player and a top class player.

EXERCISE ONE

Grab two of your mates to start the exercise. A and C stand 10yds apart and have a ball each, ready to act as servers.

B works first. B must run towards A who serves the ball for B to control with the chest and pass back to A. B then turns, runs to C and repeats the exercise.

Once B has worked for 30 seconds all the players rotate.

KEY FACTORS

1. Look to control the ball as early as possible.
2. Get in line with the ball.
3. Keep eyes on the ball.
4. Relax the body on impact with the ball to cushion it.

EXERCISE TWO

In this exercise there are 5 servers positioned around a 15yd square. At one side of the square there is a goal.

T starts in the middle of the square. S1 serves first, throwing the ball in the air towards T. T must control the ball with the chest and try to shoot past the goalkeeper, as soon as T has shot on goal they must prepare for the next serve from S2.

Once T has received a ball from every server the players rotate positions - the same key factors apply.

Players who can control a ball quickly, putting the ball in a position for a shot or pass, give themselves and their teammates the extra valuable seconds required in today's intense style of play.

49

ADULTS

Which other Premier League club has Everton boss Carlo Ancelotti previously been in charge of?

11 ANSWER

Who is the current longest-serving manager in the Premier League?

12 ANSWER

From which then non-league club did Leicester City sign Jamie Vardy?

13 ANSWER

England goalkeeper Jordan Pickford joined Everton from which club?

14 ANSWER

What nationality is Southampton manager Ralph Hasenhuttl?

15 ANSWER

Brighton midfielder Alexis Mac Allister plays international football for which country?

16 ANSWER

Other than Crystal Palace, which other Premier League side has Wilfried Zaha played for?

17 ANSWER

At which club was Jurgen Klopp managing before taking over at Anfield?

18 ANSWER

Which kit manufacturer produces Manchester City's 2020/21 playing strip?

19 ANSWER

What nationality is West Ham 'keeper Lukasz Fabianski?

20 ANSWER

V KIDS

What is the name of Sheffield United's home stadium?

11 ANSWER

How many teams make up the Premier League?

12 ANSWER

Who were the first club to win the Premier League title?

13 ANSWER

Which Premier League club has the nickname 'the Baggies'?

14 ANSWER

England captain Harry Kane plays his club football for which team?

15 ANSWER

Current Arsenal manager Mikel Arteta is a former Gunners player – true or false?

16 ANSWER

Who is Liverpool's captain?

17 ANSWER

Which London club play their home matches at the London Stadium?

18 ANSWER

How many clubs are relegated from the Premier League each season?

19 ANSWER

What nationality is Manchester City midfielder Kevin De Bruyne?

20 ANSWER

BOYS OF 2016

A crowd of 32,242 were inside the King Power Stadium on the opening day of the 2015/16 season to witness an impressive 4-2 victory over Sunderland as the Foxes began life under new manager Claudio Ranieri. Few, if any, would have predicted that Ranieri's men would go on to win a further 78 Premier League points and win the title with a ten-point cushion in what became the club's greatest ever season.

Leicester became surprise early season pacesetters and a 2-1 win away to Norwich City in October triggered the start of a ten-match unbeaten run that eventually came to an end with a 1-0 defeat to Liverpool at Anfield on Boxing Day.

That defeat at Anfield only served to strengthen the Foxes' belief, as they once again went on another impressive unbeaten run. A seven-match spell which saw the team collect 15 points and

52

CHAMPIONS
2015/16
LCFC

JAMIE VARDY

In a season when club legends were formed, striker Jamie Vardy was the name on most people's lips as the lively frontman's 24 Premier League goals proved the catalyst for Leicester's title triumph.

The former Fleetwood Town striker took the mantle of scoring the club's first goal of the season against Sunderland and went on to break Ruud van Nistelrooy's record of scoring in consecutive Premier League games as he hammered home an outstanding 13 goals in eleven consecutive Premier League outings.

He ended the campaign by being named the Barclays Premier League Player of the Season and was one of four Foxes' players in the PFA Team of the Year.

record memorable victories over Liverpool at the King Power and a fabulous 3-1 triumph over Manchester City at the Etihad.

Under amazing pressure and scrutiny from the watching world, Ranieri's team just kept winning as an incredible run of five straight league wins propelled them closer and closer to what was being described as a potential sporting miracle.

The Foxes were on the brink of the title when they travelled to Old Trafford on Sunday 1 May 2016. A win would have secured the crown but a Wes Morgan goal proved enough to earn a point and leave the Ranieri's side just two points away from becoming champions. The dream became reality the following evening when nearest rivals Spurs dropped two points after being held to a 2-2 draw at Chelsea. The result sparked a series of scenes the city of Leicester has never witnessed before and memories that players, staff and supporters will treasure forever.

TIMOTHY **27** CASTAGNE

POSITION: Defender   **DOB:** 05/12/1995
COUNTRY: Belgium

A full Belgian international, full-back Timothy Castagne joined the Foxes ahead of the new 2020/21 campaign from Italian side Atalanta.

With the reputation as a studious defender, Castagne also loves to get forward and play his part in attacking moves. He began his career with Genk before moving to Atalanta in 2017. His international bow for Belgium came against Scotland in September 2018.

28 CHRISTIAN FUCHS

POSITION: Defender   **DOB:** 07/04/1986
COUNTRY: Austria

Christian Fuchs enjoyed an unforgettable debut season with the Foxes by playing a major role in the club's 2015/16 Premier League title-winning campaign.

He featured 34 times in the title success and has now amassed almost 150 games for the club. The Austrian international has become a cult hero at the King Power and the experienced defender extended his stay with the Foxes by agreeing a new contract that will see him remain a Leicester player for the 2020/21 season.

LUKE 33 THOMAS

POSITION: Defender **DOB:** 10/06/2001
COUNTRY: England

Having initially joined the Foxes' Academy back in 2008, Luke Thomas has emerged as an exciting talent who can operate at left-back or in a more advanced position on the left flank.

He enjoyed an excellent 2019/20 campaign which culminated in him making his Premier League debut in the 2-0 victory over Sheffield United at the King Power in July 2020. He ended the season with three first team outings and being voted the development squad's Player of the Season.

ELDIN 35 JAKUPOVIC

POSITION: Goalkeeper **DOB:** 02/10/1984
COUNTRY: Switzerland

Having initially joined the Foxes from Hull City on a three-year contract in the summer of 2017, Swiss goalkeeper Eldin Jakupovic agreed a new one-year extension to his stay at the King Power in the summer of 2020.

The form of first choice 'keeper Kasper Schmeichel has limited the Swiss international's opportunities but he remains a valued and experienced member of the City squad.

JARGON BUSTER

Here is a list of footy jargon. All but one of the terms are hidden in the grid...

...can you work out which is missing?

All To Play For

Back Of The Net

Bags Of Pace

Big Game Player

Box-To-Box

Class Act

Derby Day

Dinked In

Early Doors

Funny Old Game

Game Of Two Halves

Handbags

Hat-Trick

Hollywood Pass

Keep It Tight

Massive Game

Midfield General

Natural Goalscorer

Row Z

Worldy

```
A S M Z U C E M A G E V I S S A M
V A W T B X O W A C V T S V Y B N
P O I B Y D I N K E D I N B R Q A
R L Q C J K X Z E F M L F J N E T
O G F W K C I R T T A H C S A Z U
E X B H D A V A P N H X G B J E R
T K A L L T O P L A Y F O R D C A
I R C P M E Q M O L R X G H O A L
F L K D N U R A S T T P K Q C P G
U F O N Z Y D I W O M W Y I B F O
N H F W Z O E S B B U N E H L O A
N J T G O B N O D F F X K A D S L
Y Z H S V R X M A G V O R N I G S
O X E A D C L H H G A E U D Z A C
L B N K Q J L D C J N K A B I B O
D D E R B Y D A Y E E S P A L B R
G W T E U O I P G J I O J G S M E
A C I O K I R D Y U X K T S F A R
M H W V Y B L T B P C H F O R R A
E O P C D E E T G E G Q B L P E N
V G C M I H A F M I E K Y V Z G L
H J B F D W A R T X I D H D C T D
L X D M O A S T A S O L G A T C R
V I A Q K Y I H S O D W J H Y A Q
M P F E Z P R G R G U N F M I S G
Z I N Q E J N S L J P I K Z Y S O
D B S E V L A H O W T F O E M A G
E K T X S L T E M X K W U L L I
U S N Q L U W E A B V R S P C O
A Y O R S F I T W Y O T A N B M
H O L L Y W O O D P A S S U T I
```

ANSWERS ON PAGE 62

AYOZE PEREZ

30 DAY

Day 1
Right let's get started! 10 squats, 25 star jumps, 10 sit-ups - all before school!

Day 2
Make your mum a brew before going out to practice your keepy-uppies

Day 3
10 squats
50 star jumps
10 sit-ups

Day 4
How about swapping the crisps in your lunchbox for an apple?

Day 5
Take a one mile ride on your bike

Day 6
75 star jumps
15 sit-ups
15 press-ups

Day 7
Help clean the car before going out to play headers and volleys with your friends

Day 8
75 star jumps
15 sit-ups
15 press-ups
Before and after school now!

Day 9
Walk to school rather than take the bus

Day 10
Head to the swimming pool for a 30-minute swim

Day 11
100 star jumps
20 sit-ups
20 press-ups
Twice a day now, don't forget!

Day 12
Make sure you trade one of your fizzy drinks for a glass of water today

Day 13
Jog to the shop for your mum... before playing any video games!

Day 14
Give a hand around the house before kicking your ball against the wall 500 times

Day 15
Time to increase those exercises!
25 squats
25 sit-ups
25 press-ups
Before and after school!

Day 16
Take a nice paced two-mile jog today

Day 17
25 squats
150 star jumps
25 press-ups
Remember, before and after school

Day 18
Cycle to school rather than rely on the bus or a lift

Day 19
30 squats
150 star jumps
30 press-ups
Twice a day too!

Day 20
Get out and practice those free-kicks, practice makes perfect remember...

Day 21
Get peddling! Time for a two-mile trip on two wheels today

Day 22
Upping the workload now...
40 squats, 40 sit-ups
40 press-ups
Before and after school!

Day 23
Wave goodbye to the chips - ask for a nice salad for lunch today

Day 24
40 squats
40 sit-ups
40 press-ups
Twice a day, don't forget...

Day 25
Time to get pounding the streets - the jogging is up to three miles today

Day 26
45 star jumps
45 sit-ups
45 press-ups

Day 27
Time to swap those sweets and biscuits for some fruit

Day 28
45 star jumps
45 sit-ups
45 press-ups

Day 29
You're getting fitter and fitter now! Keep up the squats and star jumps plus join an after-school sports club - ideally football!

Day 30
Well done - you made it!
50 squats, 50 sit-ups and 50 press-ups!
These are the core ingredients to your success

CHALLENGE
to improve your all-round footy fitness!

Can you figure out what ball is the real one in each photo?

WHAT BALL?

ANSWERS ON PAGE 62

JAMES
MADDISON

ANSWERS

PAGE 16 · ADULTS V KIDS

Adults

1. Conor Coady. 2. Arsenal, Chelsea, Manchester City and Manchester United. 3. Derby County. 4. Roy Hodgson, Crystal Palace. 5. AFC Bournemouth. 6. Sporting Lisbon. 7. Gillingham. 8. Four – Blackburn Rovers, Liverpool, Manchester City and Manchester United. 9. Arsenal. 10. Frank Lampard, Chelsea.

Kids

1. Liverpool. 2. German. 3. Five – Leeds United, Manchester United, Newcastle United, Sheffield United and West Ham United. 4. Wolverhampton Wanderers. 5. Manchester United/Old Trafford. 6. Manchester City. 7. The Toffees. 8. Newcastle United. 9. Sean Dyche. 10. Portuguese.

PAGE 20 · WHO ARE YER?

1. James Justin. 2. Marc Albrighton. 3. Jamie Vardy. 4. James Maddison. 5. Kasper Schmeichel. 6. Nampalys Mendy. 7. Youri Tielemans. 8. Harvey Barnes. 9. Ayoze Perez. 10. Çağlar Söyüncü.

PAGE 40
CLASSIC FANTASTIC ⟶

CLASSIC FANTASTIC

PAGE 43
SPOT THE DIFFERENCE ⟶

SPOT THE DIFFERENCE

PAGE 50 · ADULTS V KIDS

Adults

11. Chelsea. 12. Sean Dyche, Burnley. 3. Fleetwood Town. 14. Sunderland. 15. Austrian. 16. Argentina. 17. Manchester United. 18. Borussia Dortmund. 19. Puma. 20. Polish.

Kids

11. Bramall Lane. 12. 20 teams. 13. Manchester United. 14. West Bromwich Albion. 15. Tottenham Hotspur. 16. True. 17. Jordan Henderson. 18. West Ham United. 19. Three. 20. Belgian.

PAGE 56 · JARGON BUSTER

Big Game Player

PAGE 60 · WHAT BALL?

TOP: Ball F.
BOTTOM: Ball B.